Pipeline to Wealth

Pipeline to Wealth

॰ఌ

By Cheryl Butterworth

**Butterworth
Publishing**

Butterworth Publishing

Copyright 2012 by Cheryl Butterworth

Butterworth Publishing

67007-5111 Northland Drive NW
Calgary, Alberta
T2L 2L2
Canada

Toll Free Phone: 1-855-343-3330

ISBN (softcover):   978-0-9879430-2-6
ISBN (ebook):   978-0-9879430-3-3

Cover: Kamal Singh
Text: Cheryl Butterworth
Edit: Bound Publishing

ACKNOWLEDGEMENTS

I would like to thank

Trudy and **Evelyn** for their encouragement and brainstorming.

Raymond Aaron for his mentorship

Leasha West for friendship and her excitement, words and branding insights and finding me some of those wonderful Texans and being ONE!

Debra Ross for her expertize and friendship and advice on how things really work in the oil patch

Shawn Shewchuk for his invaluable coaching!

Todd Dean for putting it all together in an IT form

Michael Matthew for listening and coming up with good headlines.

Lori Murphy for being "The Book Architect' and keeping things on time and getting The Book done!

Carol Lee for her gentle and beautiful way of making you feel very special!

Theresa Weir 'The Bobsy Twin' and my Accountability Coach

A huge 'Thank You' for without each of you, this would not have come into being.

Dedication

I dedicate this book to two Women in my life who
have loved me from the beginning!

Trudy and Evelyn

FOREWORD

I have found over the time I have known Cheryl that in everything she writes, her essence shines through. Her unique writing skills and vivid imagination give you a lot of useful information, peppered with bits of humor and interesting insights, both in her self-improvement books and in her children's books.

This book is a must if you want to start your business. Cheryl is totally realistic about what you need because she is tired of the gurus giving you false hope. Reality and honesty are her platform. Integrity is one of the first words that come to mind when I think of Cheryl.

Cheryl's books and courses are written to make a difference in your life and in the lives of those around you. She has a way of simplifying and ordering what she teaches, so it is easy and enjoyable to follow.

She realizes that after a busy day at work, too much verbosity and technical jargon can put you off. She knows you'll just put the book down, along with your dreams and goals, to turn on the television. 'What a shame!' she says! She wants to motivate you to become the person of your Dreams! How better to do it? To make it easy and enjoyable. If it is too hard and unattainable, your gifts that the world needs will be lost. Your journey begins with this book and this website www.ASecondOpportunity.com

—**Raymond Aaron**
NY Times Bestselling Author
www.UltimateAuthorBootcamp.com

CONTENTS

Chapter 1:   Where is the Oilfield? Wildcatting!   **1**

Chapter 2:   Where to Drill? Finding the Right Place!   **11**

Chapter 3:   The Rig Set-up—There is an Order   **19**

Chapter 4:   Down and Dirty—It is not Always
              Easy and Clean   **25**

Chapter 5:   Roughneck—head down and Focus!   **31**

Chapter 6:   Partnering—When Funding Gets
              Low Before the Flow!   **37**

Chapter 7:   Finding Markets—NO Markets—
              NO Income—NO Need for Flow   **47**

Chapter 8:   Making Sure You X-ray Those
              Pipes—Costly Problems   **55**

Chapter 9:   Wow! You are Generating Oil!
              You can't Stop the Flow!   **63**

Chapter 10:   Cleaning up the Site—Giving Back!   **69**

WHERE IS THE OILFIELD? WILDCATTING!

There is Oil—You just have to find it

Starting a business is very much like looking for oil. The way an oil company goes about searching for oil takes many steps before they actually find and produce oil. If you compare your product or business to the product of oil, you'll find there are many similarities.

Oil companies send out seismic crews to search for oil. You will be searching the terrain that suits your gifts and talents, something that you are very passionate about. Oil companies have a passion for making money. That is the driving force for the oil industry. Everyone working within the industry believes they deserve a very high wage, which they probably do. If you're working in the field it is hard work and worth high wages, if you work in the office, it is very strenuous mentally, also deserving a high wage. In your business if you put in the time and the effort and you have a unique product or service you too, will deserve a larger reward.

What do seismic crews look for? They look for different rock formations that would indicate the likelihood of finding oil or gas. Seismic operations are sonar, meaning their machines send out sound waves that bounce back to show what lies deep beneath the surface. When you are searching for your passion, it can often be hidden deep beneath the surface. So, you quietly probe deep within to find what would light a fire within you. The fire that makes you want to get up in the morning, the fire that fire that will allow you to push on when others, that do not have your passion, would give up.

It is very necessary to work with passion, as work will become play, so that you enjoy every moment. Passion is something that goes far beyond liking something or doing something, if you could, you would spend all your time doing this thing called 'your passion' because it makes you feel good!

Talents and gifts also help you often find your passion. Talents are tendencies that you are born with, they seem to be intertwined in your DNA (the life coding molecules, that have your entire make up in each cell of your body). So talents are things that come naturally to you and to begin with are on the 'easy' side of things or you just understand how to do them. These talents are easier for you to do than for those who are not talented in them, and if you practice them or do the tasks that involve your talents repeatedly, you become more proficient at them. Skills on the other hand, are not things that come to you at birth, they are not part of your makeup, they are things that can be learned, when you have learned a skill, you may do it so well that people may even say you have a real talent doing that skill! Again with practice of a skill you also can become very proficient. Passion is essential but sometimes Passion is not enough! I know I said what you really need is just passion, but you have to consider your gifts and talents, because if you're not talented or gifted in certain areas, it may not matter how much passion you have, you may not be able to accomplish what needs to be accomplished. But saying that, if have passion for what you want done and you're able to dream or envision what you want done and explain your vision to others, so that others capture your enthusiasm and your vision, you are then able to delegate the things that you do not have the talent or skill to do, to a person who does them well, then you may stand back and watch your dream or vision come true.

What are Your Talents and Skills

What talents do you have that put you I the 'zone'? You ask 'What is the 'zone'? The 'zone' is where you are 100% hands on and focused on what you are doing, time stands still, yet it flies by, it is a place or state where time does not exist. You are so wrapped up in what you are doing you do not want to stop. Talents are things that come naturally to you; you like to do them because they <u>are</u> easy for YOU! I stress this because not everyone will find them easy, and we sometimes give too little weight or praise to what we do because of our tendency to think if it is easy for us, it is not worth much and any one can do it. Do Not Sell Yourself Short! Talents are a gift, for you to use wisely, not flaunted or given away with no regard. Talents and Skills only come from working on them and both take hard work, this type of hard work is very enjoyable, because of the enjoyment factor and you see **results** in the end!

Oil Companies, also have talents, it is their secret sauce! They specialize in doing one thing in the oil patch and in doing so can demand large amounts of funding for their specialty and exclusiveness.

Now do you see how valuable your talents are? Yes, you must share them, as they are an intrinsic part of what the world needs. They must benefit everyone, you included! Do not give away your secret sauce! But, what you need to do is share it! You say 'The Oil Industry does not share its secret sauce, why should I?' You will be sharing and being rewarded for your insights, knowledge, gifts and talents. When you are very wealth and a philanthropist you may give it away, but when you reach that place of power, you will ask that what you are giving away, those who are benefitting and using your knowledge and talent, will pay it forward and give to those who are in need, to make those who have very little in life, a life that is a bit better and easier.

Skills are learned and are different to talents because they are learned. The more you do things the better you become at doing them. Many companies have the skills needed for the tasks within a niche, so it is the quality of the skill that counts. Yes, you can be very good at what you do, and some would say you might even be talented with a set of skills, but you must learn these, you are not born with them, they are not part of your DNA makeup! Skills, too, are very valuable; the better at what it is you do, the more rewards and the more you can charge in a contract. The more talented and skilled you are, the bigger the problems you are able to solve. Companies have 'Problems' make sure you are their 'Problem Solver'! As with a Company in the oil patch, if it excels in their field of expertise or service, it can almost ask what ever amount it wants on the contract.

So if you have talents and skills that are needed in the field you desire to work within, you can ask top dollar (or whatever your currency is) for the services you render. Always give your 110% in everything you do, as you will be rewarded for your effort. Go the extra 10% and only charge for the 100%. You may not see this in the beginning, but as time goes by, people notice your attitude and your work ethics, and your advertising and marketing are being taken to individuals one at a time by word of mouth. There is no better advertising than this, it is free, yet it is priceless!

What Are You Passionate About?
Can you think about something you are not passionate about? How much effort do you put into doing this passionless task? Not Much, I would think your answer would be. So, <u>Why</u> would you do it? Did you know there are others in the world that enjoy doing those things, you dislike or are unable to do? There is only one word for it..... Delegation!!!! Delegation is where you can find someone, who really enjoys doing

the task you are not good at, or it takes too much of your time that you can use more wisely doing something else.

Think of a man who is passionate about watches, now this man is a very large man with a very large bone structure, his hands are the size of meat platters, his fingers are very thick, yet he loves and has a passion for watches and loves to see them in working order. This man would love to fix the watches, but alas his finger would not allow him to do such delicate work, what he is able to do is delegate the delicate work to someone with smaller fingers that are very dexterous. He may be able to mastermind with this other man and share insights and ideas he has about watches. In doing so each of these men benefit, by the fact that, one man saw how delegation could help him.

There have been many decades where, you were told you could do anything. I believe it was even more than 'could' but it was <u>should</u> do everything! When we did not know how to fix the leaking tap in the kitchen, we bought a book on plumbing, or even better we took a course! Then the lights needed fixing, instead of just putting a new light bulb in, we went out and got a new fixture, needing a new book or course to finish the task, it goes on and on. Or the man who had a big tree in his yard that needed to be taken down, went out bought a book and a chain saw and went to work. Can you see what is going to happen here? More books on construction, because the tree fell on the house. How much more efficient delegating would be, by giving the work to a professional, who love what he does!

So what are you passionate about? Think about it for a few minutes.

Have you come up with your passion? The thing you would like to do every day of your life? Something that could consume hours of you time everyday yet it seems you have just started and it is already time to go home? This is being in the 'zone'. How often are you in the 'zone'? How often would you like to be in the 'zone'? It all starts with finding your passion. When your work is your passion, it is like each day is play time! When was the last time you woke up early because you couldn't wait to start your day because it was just so exciting? I have been in this 'zone for a long time! Life is sweet, it was not always this way for me, I would not want to wake up and when I did, I definitely did not want to get up to face the day. I was not living my passion; I had almost forgotten what passion was. When you do not live your passion, nothing happens, you plod along, dragging one foot to the front then the next, it is like the death march, and that is just what it really is, because on the inside your soul is dying because the food it lives off of is **passion**. SO FIND YOUR PASSION!

There is no Oil, If you can't see a Gusher!

What is a Gusher? When you find oil it spews out of the top of an oil well derrick! It is something that cannot be controlled to begin with—it just keeps coming until it is capped off, but the pressure is such that capping it off when it first blows out of the ground, is almost impossible. So if there is not gusher, there is not oil... move on, keep looking, you may have to go deeper, wider or in a completely different field.

Now your passion is likened to the gusher of the oil well... if you cannot see the passion being almost uncontrollable then this is not the well site that you need to be perusing, you may have to go deeper or wider or get into a completely different field. There is nothing wrong with admitting that maybe you have made a mistake about your passion and that you don't really have enough of it to live in the 'zone' for a little while let alone forever! This is the perfect time to admit this so you do not waste anymore of your time. Look for that passion that gives you all the time in the world, life is too short not to be doing exactly what you love to do, what suits your talents and that you are skilled at doing. Life is hard enough, without making it almost impossible by doing that which you are not passionate, not talented and skilled to do. The analogy would be taking the smallest kayak with a very small plastic paddle and try to paddle it up the Niagara Falls in a couple of hours!

I hope this has been food for your thought, and if you are paddling in the wrong place, if you are drilling in the wrong field, if you are not happy with where you are, find a way out as quickly as possible. Do not waste any more of your potential or let any more opportunities pass you by.

The Opportunities—Lay Hidden (Under Fear)

Oh, the Opportunities! Some people never see them. These would be like the people who live on top on an oil field and never realize what was just beneath them. Opportunities are everywhere, but it takes a good eye to see them, then it take a brave heart to act on them, and after that it take action to make it work. If you need to be able to see an opportunity go to www.ASecondOpportunity.com there you will find many for your picking. Opportunities do not have to be grossly expensive, but they can be, but there you will find a variety of very exciting business opportunities that could be just what you have been looking for. These I know, as I have tried and tested them and found with a little work, and socializing they can be very profitable. I have a passion for each one. You can choose one to run with. Stop running after those who tell you 'Only 3 or 6 click and you will be making millions'. Remember... we are still at the searching for oil stage! Once you go through the stages, as an oil company does, you too will start to see the flow of funds into your bank account, as the oil company sees oil flowing through the pipeline. The process takes time. The ground work is extremely important; each step is the ground work for the next one. But if you are working within your passion, it will take less time than you can imagine!

Are you ready for a change? Are you tired of life the way you have been living it? This is the time for you to take that leap of faith and start living your passion!

2

WHERE TO DRILL? FINDING THE RIGHT PLACE!

When you find the oilfield—that is just the start
The seismic crew has found what they think is oil with all their calculations. Now, this is just a start to the next step! Yes, there are many steps. If followed, you will reach the destination you have been aiming for. That is Success!

In your world, you have sent out all the sound waves and they have come back saying 'This is the place to drill as there is oil there, by all the information gathered.' This is why it is so very important to gather information that is going to tell you the things you need to know, that will help you find the customers and eventually clients that will stay with you for the life of your business. If the information on the demographics is aligned to the profile of your business, and there are enough people within a certain radius of your business or you have done what is needed with your SEO and it has been correctly installed on your website, so that worldwide clients can find you easily, then you will find when you drill for this oil called 'customers', when this information reaches their ears, the pressure is going to build and your business is going to have a 'Wildcat Experience'. This is when the oil well blows! Sometimes it feels like it is taking forever! But when it blows, it is almost unbelievable! You had better be ready! As you read on you will find how the oil industry deals with this wonderful experience! Start talking to people who have had this experience, ask how they dealt with success. I cannot stress this enough, because you become almost a celebrity overnight, you may think that you can handle it by yourself, but I suggest you get a very good coach or mentor to help you through this phase of your business building.

Seismic Activity—Looking Deep into the Unknown

Seismic Activity can't be seen, you cannot touch, smell or taste it, you can only hear it, if you are at the seismic machine, and when the machine does it calculations and draws a diagram of what is below, you get to see what no other has, something from the deep, covered over for millions of years! It shows you something of the unknown, a mystery.

The same can happen when you start to research for where you can find clients, they are a hidden commodity, yet if you ask the right questions, you can find the right people who will come and frequent your business, whether you are a real store front or website. Probing and scouring for this information is going to make getting off the ground with your business a lot easier, as you will be able to target these people with the right advertising and marketing. You have to know who your customers and clients are, what their likes and dislike are, what their personalities are, the better you know <u>exactly</u> what they want, the easier it is to put yourself into their shoes, enabling you to ascertain exactly what they will buy. When you get there you will be able to feel and vision what they really want, not what you think they might want. Knowing is paramount. Think about it, if someone wants to buy you a very special gift and they have no idea who you are or what your likes and tastes are, what is the likelihood they will get you exactly what you would desire? Not really very high. Sometimes it is like trying to find something special for someone who has everything. You have to know that person inside out to put your finger on their pulse, to see or feel when the heart rate takes that leap, sometimes it is just the slightest rise, you have to be so attuned to your clients, that you can sense it without even touching their pulse. This is called 'Your Passion'. It is just a knowing, because you are in the '**zone**'! What a wonderful place to be!

Getting a Second Opinion—Getting A Coach

In the oil field, seismic charts can sometimes lack in exactness. Yes, they are usually quite accurate, but not 100% of the time. So, there are times where oil companies drill wells and hit nothing. They move over a few hundred feet and again hope for the best! Sometimes they hit oil sometimes they have another dry hole. I know this has happened on our land a number of times. It can become very expensive and more than disheartening!

In the business world, things can happen just like as above mentioned in the oil patch. How often have you set up your 'rig' and drilled hitting nothing—no customers or clients? I remember going to a weekend business fair, I had thought I had done the 'seismic mapping' for this event! But, the organizers had blatantly told some untruths, like the quality of customer (meaning the income of the household of those who would be visiting the event), and the numbers of customers that would come to the event. It was rather a game after the first day and a half, up until then it was just hard slogging. For the next day and a half, I played a game of giving a price reduction, and finally trying to give away my product. That weekend I was not successful at even giving away a pair of very high quality mohair socks! I tell you this so you are aware that you need your demographics right and spot on. You need someone to advise you, someone to coach you, someone who has been there before you. Before you sign on the dotted line, run it past your coach and mentor! Talk to people who have dealt with the people you are going to deal with, and if they tell you something that does not sound very positive to you, do not go ahead and pursue this venture.

What I am trying to tell you is to listen to people who have been there, people who are successful, people you trust. I am not telling you to talk to those around you that are still sitting on the sofa, watching

TV all night, telling you what you are doing is crazy and that you will lose your shirt, and the economy is so bad, and on and on, the nay-sayers, those who are a bit jealous of those who will show them up for what they are, on the lazy side!

Get yourself a very good coach one who is transformational, one who can get you out of your box and show you where the oil is! Don't waste your time trying to figure it all out yourself! Good and precise tools are a workers best friend, the better your tools and machinery, the easier your job becomes. You are a 'Business' worker and what you need for the job at hand is a superb coach, the best you can afford, as the advice you will receive will be invaluable! It will give you back a hundred fold!

Talking the Plan Through

Those in the oil companies head offices talk their plans through; making sure everything is thought out. Strategic planning at every level, so each division of the company knows exactly what is to happen and the next step to take. There is no guess work! It has been gone through over and over, and this is done at each level of the company, so that everyone is very clear as to what the next step will be. The oil company will send out written directives, as to what they have talked about so that there is no question as to what to do, no second guessing if you forgot what was said. It is rather iron clad, with no room for error. Errors are very costly, especially in the oil field.

Being in business is no different to the oil companies; both need very plain and solid directives as to how to go ahead. It matters not how big the company is. Even if you are the only person working on your company at the moment (if you follow all the steps, then you will have others in your employment!). You will definitely, without question, need rules, regulations and directives when you have employees. The more you plan, the smoother the operations will be, the fewer headaches you will have when, or if, someone decides their plan is better, ending up costing the company a small fortune. There is no room for egos or people who do not know how to work in teams. Another little word of wisdom for you at this point, only hire 'A' players for your team. An 'A' player will do the work of 3 'B' players and will be happy doing it. They will not cost as much as 3 'B' players all put together and it will take half of the time to get the job done! (That is my little coaching for you!)

Gridding the Oilfield—The Blue Print

There are many aspects to an oil field and to business. Each aspect in the oil field needs a different gridding map for each characteristic such as structure, thickness, porosity, permeability or saturation, so many maps are needed to get a true picture of the site and what conditions they will run into when drilling.

In business, instead of the structure, thickness, permeability etcetera you will be mapping out demographics such as age, household income, districts with in cities, customs and cultures of different countries especially if you are working on the internet. When you start mapping out these areas, you can target your marketing to suit the people you want to reach with your products or services. When you get finished doing this to begin with, it may feel like you have died and arrived in heaven! Because it will work! Just remember that this is an ongoing task you must do, as things are always changing, maybe not much but even if it changes 1 degree, you will be off course and not hit your target and not get the sales or clients you need, want and desire. Happy mapping and hunting! My, you are coming along well, there is a lot to remember but after you have done it once it will be like an old hat!

3

THE RIG SET-UP— THERE IS AN ORDER

Staking out and Fencing off the Site

When an oil company is ready to start the process of drilling an oil well, there are many things that have to happen. First of all is securing the site on which the rig and site office will be situated. They fence the perimeter of the property that they have leased from the landowner.

The area needs to have roadways built on and to it from the main road, with a gate and most likely a Texas gate so that when the oil workers are coming and going and the gate is open, cattle and other animals do not come on site. Then at the end of the day the last person off the well site closes and locks the gate, so the site is secure from animals, vandals and theft.

Business has its own parameters that have to be safeguarded. There is the outside of the building, if you have a physical location, and a front and back door that can be locked so that all inside is secure. For those who will have their business on the internet, you need

a domain name (www.TopOneDomain.com) and a
hosting package with a very good firewall. Over the
internet you need protection of those who would try
to hack your site, and others who are devious and vi-
cious sending viruses to disrupt and destroy your files
and hard drive. Make sure you have a security program that looks out for these things and stops them
before getting into your computer and causing havoc!
Make sure that every part of your business has been
secured so you are not compromised. Things happen
that are not caused by man and for no real reason,
such as a few months ago my hard drive crashed for
no reason, it was less than a year old, and the external
hard drive that I was using to back things up, was not
working! May I suggest, you have a backup hard drive
(make sure it is working properly) and a cloud account
(which is off site and you can access it at any time form
anywhere). It will save you time and heartache, should
your computer die like mine did! Please don't think it
will never happen to you! I do hope it does not but be
safe not sorry, for the extra few dollars (or whatever
currency you use) a year, you can sleep well at night
knowing in the morning all your data will be safe.

Bringing in the Site Office

The site office is where all the day to day data is kept
and then sent on to head office. This is where all the
paperwork is completed for the site. This is the place
where the directives for the site come from. This is the
hub of the whole site.

In Business the office is your equivalent. You need
a desk, a phone, fax, a printer, label machine (if you

like order and congruency—everything looking the same, then this is a must!), filing cabinets, file hangers and file folders. Some shelving for books and binders, make sure you have plenty as there is nothing worse than books and binders laying everywhere and you are not able to find what you want quickly. You will need a very comfortable desk chair for you and a chair or two for those who come to visit the office. Then there is the computer, everyone has their preference, some like PC's others are Apple people, it does not matter which you have, for each have their own benefits and idiosyncrasies. The choice is yours!

You will need stationary and business cards (after a time of being in business, the new calling or business card is a book that you write about your business), invoices and statements and other forms that are required for your particular business. Oh my goodness, I just about forgot the coffee pot!

Bringing in the Oil Rig

Bringing in the oil rig is a statement to those who are anywhere near the site. Big trucks, the rig in many pieces, stacks of pipe (for drilling the well) the list is almost endless, as there are many things needed when drilling a well.

I would liken this part of business to starting your marketing and advertising. Letting people know who you are, what you do and when you are going to be open for business. This is the set up for the start of your business, above was the physical office and supplies needed and this 'the statement of you and your purpose'. It is very important for the people to get to know YOU. They need to have a relationship with you, they need to feel comfortable with your ideals, and they need to know that you will be true to your word. You will have to build your trust with them. Relationship Capital is the most important Capital you can have. Financial Capital is great but it will not last unless you have Relationship Capital, and you can only get it by building relationships with your customers, who will then become your clients! You may think this will be difficult, but in actuality, it is fun, because you are able to talk to them about your 'Passion'!

Other Machinery for the Job

Diamonds! They always impress me. When you find them on the drill bits, they still impress me! The use of diamonds on the drill bits helps the drill go through very hard rock, diamonds are much harder than the rock it is going through, so the drill bit does not wear down as quickly as other softer materials (harder than the rock but softer than the diamonds). The cost of these bits is very high but weighing the cost of many bits that would need to be used of the softer material and the down time pulling the bit up the drilling shaft to change the bit for a new sharper one, in itself is extremely costly. So, Diamonds are forever! Is that not what James Bond said?? Or is it 'Diamonds are a girl's best friend? Or maybe it should be a Driller's best friend?

In business, there are pieces of machinery or tools that are needed for that particular business, a Chiropractor and a message therapist have special tables for their patients, a Picture Framer has specialized matt cutters and molding cutters, a Baker has mixers and ovens suited to his sort of baking. Each business has its own specialized equipment. The equipment should be the best quality you can afford, as it will pay off in the long run as it will last longer and be more precise giving you a better end product faster, instead of fighting with something that is of an inferior quality wasting your time energy and effort.

Setting up the Site and Erecting the Rig

Setting up the rig is a very tedious job, as each nut and bolt has to be put in place, one at a time and be secured so as not to come loose with any vibration from the drilling. The men that set up these rigs have a stressful job, knowing if they miss not making sure each bolt has been secured properly it could mean someone's life. Working on the rigs is a dangerous occupation (remember I said working in the field was hard work and they deserved high wages? Well, it is not just hard work but very dangerous. So yes they deserve every dollar—maybe even more!)

The site is set up in an orderly fashion, the site office will be a certain distance from the rig, and the pipe will be close to the rig for ease and speed of handling getting it to the rig's deck. The other pieces of equipment are placed on site so that each of the people working at the site knows exactly where it is, so when needed all someone needs to say is 'I need_____.' and it is on its way, no need fumbling or searching for it, because it is where it is supposed to be, now that is order!

Business should be the same, everything in order! Time is not wasted looking for things if they have a certain place and you know exactly where to find it. This is where, when you hire staff, make sure they are 'A' players, as you are assured that they will find the best place for everything or know where you find things most convenient and make sure they are always placed there, so everyone can find them. A good secretary will also have a filing system that she or he will be able to find everything, and even better, you, the CEO, will be able to find everything as well, if for some reason the secretary is away from the desk and you need something quickly!

The Office is where business is going to take place, so must run as smoothly as possible, there is no room for dramas, no room for loose cannons, it must work like a well-oiled machine, to get the most pleasure out of what you love—'Your Passion'. Do not let anyone take your passion away, but if this is the case then you have to let the crazy maker go. No Excuses!

4

DOWN AND DIRTY—IT IS NOT ALWAYS EASY AND CLEAN

Who said it was going to be Easy?

Nothing is ever really easy. Setting up an oil well site is not easy; working on the deck of the rig is definitely not easy. Yet, it appears to be easy when an untrained eye is looking on. People make things look easy because they have been doing it for so long. They have built up the muscles and skills, while working with the pipes and bits. Working on the rigs is dirty! There is no way of getting around it, as you are pretty close to being a grease monkey, I know it is an automotive term but somehow conjures up a good picture of the oil and grease that someone working in that environment gets into.

In business it is not easy either! But when you have a passion for what you are doing, it is easy because you are enjoying it. You have a talent and a skill that most people do not have, so it look easy from the outside only because you have done the task so many times that is just comes naturally. Sometimes the things we must do to get things started and moving, takes a bit of dirty work and you may have to get your hands dirty. It is okay if you have the funds to delegate these jobs to those who enjoy the work and are talented doing them. But, if you really want to know how the business works from the ground up, and to know how long things take to do, how difficult they may be, then it is imperative to do it all at least once! I know people do not like to do those things that they don't have the talent or skill to do, but it builds character and give you an appreciation for those who do those tasks!

Three Clicks to a Million is just a Con!

Just as much as you wish this could be true, it is not! Anything worth a million takes more than three clicks! Even those who are being paid high wages in the oil patch, do not get paid a million, and what they do I can assure you, is more than three clicks!

Do not be conned any longer, do not pay your hard earned cash to another 'guru' of any sort, because these people are conning you. They tell you how lucky you are to have found them as they are multi-millionaires and they are wanting to give back, that they are mad at all the other gurus, but they are all the same vying for your dollars, first with a small amount to draw you in, then a bit bigger amount, just because you really need this and the first program they sold you isn't worth the money you spent on it, but then they do not let you leave the site without trying to sell you a very expensive program and if you don't buy it, they will make you feel guilty and infer because you did not buy it, you will never make the Big Money without it! But when you finally buy this last piece of the puzzle, you realize all too late that there is a flaw in it somewhere and it really does not work and the jargon is so complex, they are trying to bamboozle you with their verbosity making them look so very clever and making you feel so very inadequate. Do not Believe all you hear!!

Getting Dirty—Getty a New Perspective

This is about getting dirty rich! It was a Freudian mistake on my part it should have been 'Getting a New Perspective' not 'Getty a New Perspective' But how sweet it is when these things happen! J. Paul Getty was one of the richest men in the U.S.A. He wrote a number of books but the one that interested me was 'How to be Rich.' Published in Chicago by Playboy Press in 1965. He was an authority on the subject to say the least! It looked like he must have been friends with Hugh Hefner.

J. Paul Getty made his first million dollars by the time he was 24 years old. During the Great Depression he added another 3 million to his estate. I find this also very interesting that one person could acquire so much during a depression while other had no money and could not find work.

This book is called 'Pipeline to Wealth'—'You don't have to be a Texan to be as wealthy as one!'

Now I do not know if you'll be as wealthy as J. Paul Getty. But I know that the news keeps saying there is a bad downturn in the economy and this has been going on since 2008. It is not called a depression as it was in 1930's. Now if J. Paul Getty was able to make a huge amount of money in the depression years, why then, could it not be possible for YOU to make a huge amount of money in this downward trend?

Let me tell you right now **'Everything is Possible'**

When I was 9 years old I had just about an hour uninterrupted, one afternoon with a man who told me a most wonderful truth, which was

'Cheryl, never let go of your Dreams, because they <u>Can</u> come true.'

This man was Walt Disney. Look at what dreams he had that came true.

No Pain—No Gain

I once had a friend who would tell me over and over 'No Pain, No Gain!'

I used to hate the saying because, I was in pain, I had done something wrong and was learning. We learn through our mistakes. We do not forget our mistakes because of the pain! But each time I learned by making the mistake, I gained great knowledge and insight. Since this time I have found out a much better way of learning these lessons, and it is called 'Genius'! You learn from other peoples mistakes. After a while you do not need the pain to learn, as you still can recall pain. And if you are wise you will have others relate to you where their downfall has been and how they dealt with it and overcame the difficulties. What a better way to learn, it is faster, more efficient and a whole lot easier than going through pain! Now, if you still need the pain for some unknown reason, by all means take the hard road, but I shall opt for the road less travelled.

What a Gush! Or is it a Rush?

Well, if you are in the oil patch it is 'What a Gush!' For when the well blows—you have a Gush! Oil spewing everywhere and that is something each person on the site gets excited about. It makes everything that has gone before all worth it! There is a bonus for everyone who is on site when it blows! Friends at the well site that can feel the well going to blow call all their friends to come quickly, that is how exciting it is, and of course there is the <u>bonus</u> also! That is if you are actually on site when it blows!

In Business, it is **'What a Rush!'** When you get your first sale, **'What a Rush!'** When you have a physical shop and the doors open the first day and there is a long line up **'What a Rush!'** When you have you first order online **'What a Rush!'** When you make your first $100,000. **'What a Rush!'** When you become a Top 1% (in Canada making $250,000. a year) **'What a Rush!'** When you make your first Million Dollars. **'What a Rush!'** When you write and publish your first book and have it in your hands for the first time. **'What a Rush!'**

Life is what we make it! We can set goals and achieve them. We can set new goals. We can choose to be happy. We can choose to be positive. We can choose to be helpful and generous. We can choose to love. And we can choose to be Grateful.

If we choose to do all these things life will be and continue to be **'What a Rush!'** I choose to live my life like this and I hope that you will follow me into this magical world of passion, for what you do. There is no better way to live. It is exciting and life is never boring, there is always something new and different to capture your imagination. If you allow your mind the time and joy of imagination, you will be amazed at the wonders it comes up with. Where do you think all the inventions come from? Yes, they come from people just like you. Happy and excited about life and what is coming next! Are you ready to rekindle your Dreams? Remember what Mr. Disney said 'Never let go of your Dreams, because they CAN come true.' Are you ready?

Information about J. Paul Getty was attained at: http://en.wikipedia.org/wiki/J._Paul_Getty

5

ROUGHNECK—HEAD DOWN AND FOCUS!

Keep Your Eyes on the Drill

The Roughnecks, or in Canada they are called Floorhands, job has to be one of the most dangerous of almost any job, and without doubt it is in the oil patch. You have to admire these men who risk their lives to find that elusive oil! These men are strong and focused! If you don't have the strength, you cannot be a roughneck as the work is very hard and manual. These fellows work on the drill floor dealing with the drills, pipe and specialized drilling equipment and pressure controls. They connect the pipe that goes down the well bore. Roughnecks can be very skilled or more of a gopher on the drilling deck.

A Floorhand also known as a "worm" is usually considered the lowest member of the drilling crew; this is the dirtiest and most physically demanding position. The Floorhand works primarily on the rig deck where he operates the tongs, iron roughneck and other equipment and does pretty much any job asked of him.

A Chainhand is a floorhand that can also throw chain, but he is the floorhand that watches out for the 'worm' and does not get as filthy.

A Toolpusher is the highest position at the drilling site, he responsible for all the crews. He stays on location for a few days or weeks at a time during operations, individual drilling crews work only eight- or 12-hour shifts.

A Driller is the head of an individual crew, with the responsibility for controlling a rig's machinery during drilling, and most other rig operations.

A Derrickhand is responsible for the drilling mud, the mud pits where drilling fluids are circulated around the system. The mud pumps are large reciprocating pumps used to circulate the mud (drilling fluid) on a drilling rig. He also acts as a lead for the driller who is mostly restricted to the rig floor.

A Motorman is responsible for maintaining engines, water pumps, water lines, steam lines and boilers. He is also responsible for moving all the equipment on site.

In business, when you start hiring employees, you will have to make job descriptions for each position, firstly, so the employee knows what is expected of them, him or her, and secondly so there is little or no overlap in the positions, yet if there is an absentee, one of the other employees would be able to cover that position for a short time.

Make sure you train your staff as to how you want thing done and how you want your company run. If not and they have worked for someone else they will be bring with them habits they learned from the last employer. If you do not train them, they are not at fault—YOU ARE!

So as the Roughneck has to keep his eyes in the drill and stay focused, you too, need to keep your eyes on your business and stay focused to make sure things keep running smoothly and you are able to counteract anything that will cause a disruption in your day to day operations.

Keep the Momentum Going

Keeping the momentum going on a drilling rig is essential, downtime is lost money! It is costly having the crews doing nothing during downtime. Head Office has calculated how long the project should take and had budgeted accordingly. Remember me telling you, the passion of and Oil Company is money! Losing money in downtime hurts the bottom line. Starting up again takes quite a while to get up to speed. In years gone by when the rigs used steam power, it would take time to get the steam up. Anything that has to be put in motion from a stand still will take more energy and effort to start the motion than if it has just slowed. So Downtime must be held at bay as much as possible.

In business it is just the same, you do not want to lose any momentum.

In some cases when things slow down, procrastination will set in, and trying to motivate staff out of procrastination is as hard as starting a stream engine from stand still into motion, it takes a lot of energy. In business it is YOUR ENERGY AND PASSION

THAT WILL BE TAXED! So avoid downtime if at all possible!

Never Stop (Down Time is Like an Oil Leak)

Downtime is like an oil leak, it doesn't look like much when it is just a drop at a time, but drips add up to puddles and then just grows! The oil lost is costly sometimes it is your profit! No one wants to have their profit being leaked out or dripped away. The problem with oil is that it is toxic to the environment and trying to clean up an oil spill is lengthy and on the extreme end of costly! So, not only do you lose your profit but you can only hope your insurance kicks in or you have made so much in the last couple of quarters to cover the bill or you do not survive! And if you should be so lucky to have the insurance company fund your oil leak, you can be assured your insurance premium will sky-rocket the next year!

In business there are leaks that are costly, like pilfering, or time at the water cooler or coffee pot, gossiping. If you have a physical shop or store, you have to make sure everything is in order and safe for your clients and staff, so as no one is at risk of injury. One law suit, because someone has tripped over the door sill, can put a small company out of business, so make sure you are well insured for such things and hope you never need use it. I am not trying to be a horror monger, but trying to make sure you are protected, that your business thrives and your passion never stops! It would be wrong of me not to tell you of different pitfalls. Once warned makes you prepared and protected.

Never Give Up—Go Back to the Coach as often as Needed

As Oil Companies do not lose their passion for money and huge profits at the end of the year, they do not give up, they just move the rig a few 100 feet away, as the seismic crew was sure there was oil there somewhere! The oil company will go back to the seismic company and ask for another seismic report of the area to pinpoint or at least come closer to where the oil may be. Remember moving one of those rigs is extremely costly. So going back to get another report may cost but not as much as moving a rig and again not finding oil in yet another hole!

In Business if you have not hit oil or your target and goal, then go back to your coach and figure out what you are doing that is not productive, or what you can do to tweak what you are doing. Remember again, when you are just 1 degree off target, you will not hit your goal, but with just a little adjustment you will get to where you want to be. If you leave it and wait or your pride gets in the way the amount of area you have to come back from is greater and will take more time, energy and definitely more money. Your coach will not charge you anything near what you are losing through, willful stupidity. Just go and see what transformational ideas will be given to you! What leaps and bounds you can make, you will be happy and so will your coach! If your coach is anything like me or my coaches, we delight in your progress and success, and we would rather nip things in the bud, rather than having to cut down a forest, because you have not wanted to deal with a small problem and have let it get completely out of control. So please do me a favor, go see or phone your coach before you get into any kind of trouble.

What happens if You Stop Drilling?

On the oil rig if you stop drilling, you get nowhere, you are not going in a forward positive motion, because you are not in any motion at all. Well, saying that maybe you are in a motion, but you are going backward, in a way you cannot see. You can't see it as it is financial and it is hidden in the books and in the numbers, and unless you are the accountant or the CEO you might not realize how fast the backward motion is taking you.

Don't stop what you are doing in business, if it is working, and if it is not working, get in touch with your coach and get your company back on track as quickly as possible. Speed is of the essence, you have no time to lose. The more time you procrastinate and tell yourself it will be okay; the further away you are getting from your goal. Again, a waste of time, energy and money, and you will have to play catch up. And do you ever really catch up... I don't think so (because all the money you are making trying to catch up would be profit if you were not catching up!!!)

Try to keep going at all costs, not losing momentum and keeping your passion, knowing you are going to succeed! I believe in YOU!

6

PARTNERING—WHEN FUNDING GETS LOW BEFORE THE FLOW!

Finance and Funding

The Oil and Gas Industry gets its financing and funding through having the company being listed on the stock market, where those investing in their stocks provides the funds for the company to grow and the funds for research and development. When bigger projects are on the table or companies want to move into other countries then mergers and acquisitions are all part of the way forward. The Oil companies have department specifically designed for these specialized negotiations. The people who they hire are top notch lawyers and negotiators; they in turn hire assistants, Land men and when dealing in other countries, translators. The Oil and Gas Industry also hire accountants that deal not only with the taxation issues but figuring out the costs and profits of new acquisitions, they also look after the running of the of the whole business.

When you start a business, often it is <u>your money</u> that makes up your start-up financial position. This is often the only way you can start. But in doing this, you will have to have a promissory note drawn up to re-compensate you for the funds you have given to your company so as to be paid back in a certain amount of time, usually 10 years, and at a high interest rate (a rate that a risk investor would be charging). This is a very fair way to get refunded, as you are risking a lot and is a tax advantage. A statistic that is worrying is for every 100 businesses that are started in a five year period, only 66 to 75 SURVIVE. That is one in three or four companies that do not make it. What I am trying to help you with, is information that will help you achieve what you are wanting, side-stepping around the pitfalls so many people fall into. Knowledge is essential to survive and thrive! When people tell you where they have failed or know place others have fallen victim to bad advice or just poor practices, please listen with great care, as these stories can save you and your business. The main reasons businesses fail is the lack of strong business management and lack of strong financial management. If you do not have a tight grip on both, the business and finances are going to slip away from you. You need to know what is happening in your business all the time, you need to know all your numbers, how much you have in the bank, how much you are owed and how much you owe. You need people who have gone before you, you need a good coach, to show you where not to go and show you all things are possible, at the right time!

I do not want to be a wet blanket, taking the shine off business, but to tell you it is easy and there are no pitfalls, I would be lying to you. But saying that I want to encourage you to go for your goal, there is nothing better than being your own boss, earning more than you could ever make working for someone else, having more time to spend how you wish, whether it is with family or on the golf course or climbing a mountain. Not many who work for others get have this kind of lifestyle. Go For What <u>YOU</u> Want!

Life is just so long, if you have not done what you wanted today, you are a day further away and you have a day less to get there! What is holding you back? What could motivate you to take that first step to be where you want to be?

Accounts

Accounts are a top priority to Oil Companies. They have an accounting department that keeps everything in order. They have to be on top of everything on a daily basis. This is how important the numbers are. They do not let anything go over a certain amount in the budgeted plan. There is a contingency of 10-15% over-run, but it cannot run over that as they will start working in the RED (In accounting terms red means in a deficit—or losing money! Remember the main objective for an Oil Company is to make money and lots of it!)

There are different kinds of accounts. Accounts receivable, being the money that is coming to the company (money other people owe the company). Accounts payable, being the money the company owes others (money the company has to pay others for services or products).

What needs to happen in every case to make a business thrive is to have more coming in or more accounts receivable than money going out being accounts payable. It sounds very simple! And it is very simple! But all too often it does not happen, and this is call poor management. If you struggle with the management of finances, there is a super course on how to manage money in a logical and easy to read and follow program from www.ASecondOpportunity.com. I highly recommend this if you do not have a firm foundation in financial matters. Business is fun and exhilarating, until you run into financial problems. Start a business with as much knowledge as possible especially financial insights, and you will enjoy what you do while building your empire! There are always ups and downs in business but if you can see the trends and act quickly to counteract before anything gets away from you and starts to be in the driver's seat taking the company (who should be in that seat? YOU!) down the road at a speed that is completely out of control. So, educate yourself, you do not have to be an accountant, but you have to know what is coming in and going out and how to make sure things stay in the proper order. Now this is called Good Management! You can delegate the work to those who do bookkeeping, accounting and tax accounting, as they know all the right things to do. The tax accountants know the tax credits that can be used to benefit the company; they keep up with their education to be able to benefit those who they are being employed by. The more education you and your employees acquire, the more smoothly and efficiently the company will be.

When you are starting your business, make sure your personal accounts and your business accounts are not mixed together. All the money you have leant the company should be recorded for later use. If your business has not been going long enough to acquire its own credit card, take one of your credit cards and designate it for the use of the company only.

Running Out of Time

Running out of Time! It is more often the Governments that help the Oil Companies run out of time! Passing bills and negotiating, things like pipeline routes in their own and different countries, takes time, sometimes years. These kinds of delays can almost destroy a company. Other tactics are often necessary to get things moving, for example with a route of a pipeline; the pipeline may have to be re- routed through a different country. At this moment Alberta is trying to negotiate a pipeline from Fort McMurray to the Pacific Ocean, having to go through British Columbia. The two Premiers do not want to budge on any issue that arises on either side. It is rather a stalemate. Alberta is looking at alternative ways to move the oil and is looking further south to Washington. Time waits for no one, no matter whom or how much money you have. It just keeps marching on, and often leaving people, businesses and governments behind and each one being a loser, because you cannot make up time. The only time I have found time can be made up is when flying and having a tail wind, putting you head of time at your destination. But in reality time does not change, only once was it recorded in history when time stood still, only once and it has not happened again. So the thought of making up time is just a fallacy, you have to start from where you are, that you have lost the time and re-calculate the time frame you have to cross your finish line.

Now, when you are going into business, there are no differences for you really than the large oil company. You may not have the government giving you a problem, but there are many ways you can run out of time. The Banks can hold you up with their internal systems and then coming back wanting more security. May I say right now, banks are not your friend. They may have many people who are nice and talk to you soothingly, passing their documents across the desk, even giving you their personal pen to sign the document. That document is putting you in bondage to the bank. Now if you are in need of more funds and go back to the bank with no more security to put up for extra funds that could keep you going, you will be refused flatly, they have no compassion, they are big business and they like the oil companies goal and bottom line is money and a lot of it. This can put you in a tail spin, trying to figure out where you can go next.

Running out of Money
Running out of money is something that is not really heard of in the oil industry. But it is there, you just don't hear about it. This is when you hear about

mergers and acquisitions to inject more money into a company so it does not fold. When a big business folds it hurts everyone and starts rumors or recessions. Other oil companies will pick up a company in trouble for cents on the dollar, so that the company does not go under, the new owners have received a good deal the old owners have been relieved of a huge burden and the employees may continue with their employment or if the new owners start with a clean slate they are most often rehired.

Banks do not really help as I started above, so this is not a place to go for help, you will just be disappointed.

Partners

Often Oil companies will partner with each other so as to benefit both companies. Sometimes one company has the expertise and the other has the money. Sometimes they both have the expertise but in different fields so that they complement each other's work and they get the job done quickly and efficiently, without problems that can come about when hiring out jobs in a piece meal fashion. You know that the other company has as high of standards as you, so you know the job will be done in a timely manner to a standard expected. When acquiring these partners, the deals are made and the lawyers go to work, drawing up papers to layout each company's duties and expectations, then the way the funds from the project will be divided. When both companies agree on the terms and conditions laid out in the documents they are signed and witnessed. If the documents are not signed there is no contract and there are no legal ties to each other. Make sure your lawyer is involved drawing up agreements, if the other party wants their lawyers to do that, and then make sure your lawyer reads the agreement and advises you to the legalities.

This is a word of warning, do not go into a partnership that is not a Limited Company, this is for your protection! Have a lawyer draw up the articles of the company and make sure he or she explains to you everything that this company and partnership involves. I made this mistake only once. It was very costly. As they say you learn by your mistakes, but a genius learns by the mistakes of others.

When you start your business, there are a few people who will be of great benefit to you and your company, they are good coach, a good corporate lawyer, a bookkeeper, and a good accountant. Take guidance from these people as they have a great wealth of knowledge that will help and protect you and your company. Please do not think you can do it all on your own. No man (or Woman) is an island, there is no shame in asking advice, on the contrary—there is shame in not asking as it can cost you your business!

Business is not for the faint-hearted, it is not always easy, but it is the most exhilarating way of life, as it gives you freedom, it gives you an income beyond anything you would ever receive by working for someone else, it gives you time that you can do what you want and when you want. It gives you a challenge; it gives you something to get up in the morning for, giving you a purpose to life. It may take a little while to get there but not that long, once you get all your ground work done, as the oil industry gets the site ready for drilling, then the business will take off! All I can do is encourage you, because when that oil well blows, the excitement is unbelievable and your life will never be the same again!

FINDING MARKETS— NO MARKETS—NO INCOME—NO NEED FOR FLOW

Marketing

The Oil Companies are experts at marketing. Tell me what you think when I say 'Tiger in your Tank'? Did you say Esso? What about the big yellow shell with red around it? Again, you most likely said Shell. What about 'the big red maple leaf with black on the left hand side'? If you do not live in Canada, you are forgiven if you do not get this one! It is Petro-Canada. You see there are symbols and logos that point our minds towards their companies and products. Now, that is good advertising. But it goes further than just that, they have a brand and they want that brand to make you use no other brand of oil but theirs. That is Brand advocacy. That is where you will not use any other kind of gas to go in your vehicle. Once a company has you there, then they are assured of 100% of your budget that goes to fill your car or truck. If they have you at brand preference, they get some of your money but not all of it; they have not sold you hook, line and sinker! I know people who believe Shell is the only gasoline to put in your auto, they will not use any other brand as they are sold on the benefits of the Shell products, so, they may even travel across town passing by 15 service stations to get to a Shell station . That is what a business wants of its customers, if they are advocates, they are clients forever (as long as your products do not change or they get better).

Marketing is one of the most, if not the most, important part of your business! If you don't have it right, you don't have a business for very long. Marketing is not just advertising, as so many people think. Marketing is not just a company logo; it is much, much, more. Marketing is being able to be seen. If people cannot see you and know what you or your company stands for, you don't even get the slightest glace from a prospective customer. It used to be if you had the right product or what people wanted in your store, people bought it. Then came the era of 'Who you know', if you knew the right people then you might get a discount or be introduced to someone who could help you. But this is the era of 'Who knows YOU'. You may not know them but it is imperative that they know you! The only way to get them to know you is through marketing! There are many different aspects of marketing, making a splash in your home town or city, or it could be on the internet using tools like Facebook, Google+ or

LinkedIn, just a few examples. You have to be branded, sometimes it is the company, sometimes it is you, and often it is both.

Go to www.Extra-OrdinaryConnections.com to find real people that excel in their professions and in this case look under 'Marketing'. This website only recommends tried and trusted companies. You see how it works? Some of these people do not know me by name or would not pick me out in a crowd but I know them, I know what they can do and what they do, they do well (extremely well!) So this is the first insight into marketing.

Where

I believe in today's market, you need to be seen at home (meaning around your town or city) and on the internet. The telephone book era has sadly passed, there is really no such thing as the white pages any more, for the exception online! I have been told phone companies will sell you a white pages book for your city at a price that is so dear very few can afford them. They want people to use the 411 number or go online to the white pages there; it is far more cost effective for the company. Big changes are happening all the time, it may not be what the majority wants in some cases, but to cut costs where necessary enables businesses to carry on and make a profit. The Telephone Company was not making a profit on the white pages, so shut the printed copy down being able to charge people to phone the 411 number and add an additional charge for connecting you to the number they have just supplied you! So, Profit is the name of the game, so where something is not making you money, revamp it so that you will be making money from it and stop how you were doing it and losing money! Take a lesson from the phone company. They too are online, as are the Oil Companies. Don't get stuck on local or on internet—you need both so get stuck on them both.

When marketing in your neighborhood, you can use billboards, direct mail flyers, or letters mailed by the post office, there are bus stop booths and benches that you can advertise on, there are posters you can put up in stores. You have your business cards, you have your brochures—but think about a book written by you, now that would be a real marketing strategy. And you the author could personally sign a copy for your prospective new client! This is one of the most cost effective ways of advertising on the market, today.

As you continue reading let that little thought sink into your subconscious, to bubble back up when you have started your business.

When you are ready, come back to

www.Extra-OrdinaryConnections.com and find people to help you write your book and brand you, then market you! Remember you are not an Island and the more help you can receive the faster, bigger and more profitable your company will become.

When

When should you market? Day and night! Do you think the Oil Companies ever stop marketing? The answer is NO! So, nor should you!

This is why the internet is so good because it never shuts down, it runs 24/7, and it is open to anyone in the world. Marketing you do in your home town is not broadcast to the world, if you use the radio, it has a radius of maybe 100 miles on a good day, on a clear night it could reach much further. But saying that, is your advertisement on during that clear night and does that person hearing it know where this is being transmitted from? Just about the time the call letters and city of the station are to be announced there is a bunch of static so your ad has been wasted in this case. Each form of marketing and advertising has its benefits and its drawbacks. It is like walking through a maze trying to figure out which path will lead you to the exit or your goal! Remember the word 'Coach'.

Both radio and television advertising are very expensive and the return is not always what you would wish for. With this kind of advertising you must find a trusted station that knows their demographics so as to guide you to knowing the best time on the airwaves your message will be heard and acted upon. Too often I have found a Charlton talking to me on the other end of a phone, wanting to sell me time on his station, with little regard for my needs but wanting to make his quota for the week. This is not the kind of person you want to deal with, you choose the station and the sales person, and if they do not suit you and your needs move on quickly before it costs you a lot of money.

Newspapers and neighborhood monthly magazines are two good sources for advertising but again you need to know when the newspaper or magazine will be read, by whom and depends on your product or service being needed. There are many variables. A coach can help you with figuring out just the right place to do your advertising. A good IT person can help get your name and company name on the internet where it is most likely to be seen and knowing where to place click ads to be the most beneficial to your company.

Why

If Oil Companies did not market, they would not find markets to sell their oil, people in the world have to be lead to finding what they want, and if you are not showing them what you have to offer, how are they going to know what you have, let alone find you? So, again marketing is getting the public, be it in your town or around the world, being able to see you and your company, so they can judge whether you are a person or company that fits into their ideals and standards, who they want to do business with. This is the day of the buyers' market, it is the buyer who decides what he wants to buy, you cannot go to the customer and sell to him, people do not like to be sold to, but rather they like to buy from. You are both doing what was done before but there is a different emphasis on how it is done. So you as the seller or business that has something to offer the world, has to put it out there for the world to find you. In doing this you have to know where and how and when and who you need to challenge with your wonderful wares or services, you have to make it as easy as possible for this public as they are fickle and have a short attention span, what you need is the right place with the right catch phrases or ads that will intrigue and draw these people into wanting to know more about you and what you are offering. The longer they stay, the more you will sell them.

Who

Who will your customers and clients be? Those who want your products or services. Oil Companies know there customers are people with vehicles that need gasoline to run them. So what products or services are you putting out there to offer? The people you are trying to reach, you will have to know their language, their like and dislikes, where they hang out, who they meet up with and converse with. If you go to different forums on the internet for the services and products you supply, you will find people who will want what you have, it may take a little time before they do buy from you as they have to get to know you, you have to be validated and you have to have some credentials before you can be trusted. Unfortunately, there are many scoundrels out there that have taken advantage of people online, so people are still a bit weary, I think you probably know someone who has been ripped off by someone like this, maybe you yourself have. So you can start to understand how your customers are feeling about you and your company, you have to show them who you are, a person with integrity or a company that stands behind what it says and what it sells. An analogy if your customers were like fish and you were the fisherman, you would have to bait the hook with something that they really liked something that was worthwhile, looked good and maybe even free to start with (this is so they can have a test drive to see if you give them what they were expecting.) And, if you do? They will become your lifetime clients! The ones you want, because they will buy everything you offer them, they love sets of things, they love your books so will buy all of them. They love your courses, so they buy all of them. When people like you and what you have to give and sell them, they will not leave you. This is what you would call a marriage in Heaven! It can't get much better.

How

The how, is started by taking one step at a time. In this way you will not overstep or leave anything out. As I have said before there is an order and if you follow it you will hit oil. If you skip steps you will not be prepared for the next level. It is like going to school and taking math classes, if you skip a grade, you miss out on the formulas that you need to figure out the next bunch of equations, if you do not have the knowledge you can't go forward, you can try but your answers come out wrong and you fail for lack of knowledge. So if you can do two years in one gaining all the mathematical secrets that is fine, because you have touched on all the steps. So speed is fine as long as you have set down your foundation, and you know where you are going. Again, to do all this as quickly as possible you need that awesome coach!

The Coach is waiting for you, and you can find him or her at www.Extra-OrdinaryConnections.com look under 'Coaches'

CHAPTER

8

MAKING SURE YOU X-RAY THOSE PIPES— COSTLY PROBLEMS

Every Pipe has its Weakness

The oil industry is alive and well in Alberta. I travelled to Edmonton earlier this week, on the highway the amount of traffic was incredible and a great majority of it was to do with the oil business. There was truck after truck hauling pipe to the north, most likely to Fort McMurray, but there are also other places in the province that has pipelines being installed. I looked on with wonder at the cost of it all. The pipes must have been 30-40 feet in length, and there must have been close to 100 plus on each truck. I have also heard it is a very dangerous job hauling the pipe, it is not the transporting of them but the unloading them at the other end, many a young man has lost his life, others have had their legs crushed by being in the direct line of the pipes escaping their moorings from the flat bed. Now you realize why wages are so very good—it is called 'Danger Pay'.

I have deviated a bit, but I think you needed that little insight. The pipes on those big trucks looked so pristine, they were white, some had bright orange caps on the ends, and the sight was impressive. The pipes had just come from a steel manufacturer who produced these awesome pieces of carbon steel. The process that goes into making one of these pipes is incredible. They start as a flat piece of steel, as the flat steel is taken from a pile of plate stock; it is given a unique identification number, this is to track this pipes performance for its lifespan. The flat steel then has its edges milled so they can be crimped (this allows the edges to be fitted together by welding and still be the same thickness as the rest of the pipe when finished); they then go to a 'U' press where they are molded into a 'U' shape. Trying to take a flat surface and make a pipe out of it in one step would put too much tension and stress on the steel and it would fracture or weaken the steel. The next stage is to put the 'U' molded steel into an 'O' press, this finally get the steel looking like a pipe. The pipe is then welded on the outside and then on the inside, the next step is inspecting to make sure the welds were solid. The outside is once again welded and goes for an ultrasonic test, then, it is X-rayed. There are more steps to be taken like expanding the pipe, this is to give more strength also giving the pipe the right thickness, and from there it goes through more testing with ultrasonic and X-ray machines and finally having the end beveled for welding in the field. The pipe is now ready to go on those trucks!

The pipe is gently placed on the flat beds, tied down securely for the long journey. Everything has been harsh but gentle for these pipes, their molding was stressful making them strong with the tempering, but the handling of the pipes has been gentle with the use of cranes and forklifts. The transportation has been smooth, riding on 36 rubber tires and an air suspended flat deck; everything seems idyllic for them until they reach their destination! When they get to the field, there are no cranes or forklifts that unload them, just that poor young driver, who pulls the strapping off them, and it is like all hell breaks loose! What a shock to these unsuspecting pipes! Will their welds hold? Who knows? I know someone who does! Her name is Debra Ross; she is the CEO of Gamma-Tech Inspections Ltd. Her company does non-destructive testing of these gentle giants in the ground or when they are just being placed in their new home. This kind of new technology is what the future needs, something that does not hurt the environment, is pro-active, looking for problems before they start to be problems, having them fixed before any damage is done to the place where they lay and assuring the precious oil being transported through them is not lost due to leakage.

This is Good Business practice, if only, all businesses were there to help solve problems as Debra Ross is, this world would be a much better place. She has taken something, an idea at first and made it work for the benefit of the oil industry, the environment, the people living near the pipelines, well, pretty much everyone benefits from what she does! She is exemplar! Do take a lesson from someone who has gone from an idea to being awarded 'The Oil Industries, Entrepreneur of 2012'. This she has done in a few short years!

What is your good idea? What is stopping you for going to make a difference in the world? You can do it! I believe in YOU!

Turning a Blind Eye and Facing the Truth

There was an oil spill in the Gulf of Mexico a few years ago. You probably remember it. The pictures in the paper, the footage on TV, the oil oozing (rather flooding) into the water, the birds that were black with the oily goo all over them, the lucky ones were caught and cleaned with detergent, the unlucky ones suffocated or drown. All this because, someone had turned a blind eye and did not want to admit anything was wrong. The oil companies can track the oil and tell you exactly where it is in the pipe, and they can tell if a few barrels are missing! So, how could this oil spill happen? Could it be someone was not doing their job? Could it be, a lot of people were not doing their job? What did this 'Blind Eye' cost? It was in the Millions! Who can account for the wildlife lost, can it ever be restored? And what is the cost of those fish and animals that no longer have a habitat to live in, that is if any of them survived!

When you are in business, do not turn a 'Blind Eye' to problems, as they are costly. Some problems like the one just mentioned would put a small business <u>OUT</u> of business! That is not why you are wanting to go into business! Remember, I said that a company fails because of a lack of two big things? They are a lack of strategic management and planning and or lack of financial management. If you have turned your back on a problem, turned a blind eye or just stuck your head in the sand saying it will go away,' Honey! You have a huge problem! The first part of the Huge Problem is **YOU**!' You have to face up to the problem as soon as you are aware of it and fix it; sometimes you need others to help you fix it! Again a word comes to mind! 'Coach'. Do not be too proud or egotistical because the fall is just too harsh for anyone to bear! It is so much easier to face the truth and deal with things quickly, sometimes it will cost but you but your integrity will be intact, and people will respect you. You have no idea how much business you will receive by doing the right thing! I know how much you would get if you kept your head in the sand! Zip, Nil, Noda and that all adds up to NOT A THING!

Now that I have your attention, 'Please walk softly and enjoy your journey!'

Being Pro-active

Being Pro-active means you are on top of things, you see things before they happen. You do maintenance, not repairs! It is far more efficient to make sure everything is in working order, if you leave things to break down or don't take the time to fix them, you will find the down time far longer and more expensive than keeping things in order! If you hire someone to be in charge of making things run smoothly, it will take a lot of stress away from you, not having to remember everything and check on all operations constantly. Just make sure the person you hire is an 'A' player, someone you will never have to babysit. Again remember we are not Islands and we need other people to help us. Getting help like this, in itself is pro-active. Being in business does not mean you are to work yourself to the bone, but it means that you are enjoying what you are doing, you have time to enjoy your activities outside of work, and you enjoy family and friends. This is not a dress rehearsal, this is the real thing, you only have one shot at it, so make it what you want it to be!

Safety—Expensive or Costly?

Oil Companies reward employees for safety records. If you have ever been on an oil drilling sight, in the field office, you would have seen, in a prominent place, a board with '____ Days Accident Free'. Everyday a new number is placed in that blank space, ever hoping it does not become a '0'. The more days they have safety freedom, the more bonuses they receive! This may sound like the company likes everyone to be healthy and well, and I'm sure they do, but the bottom line is—you guessed it! MONEY! It is costly when there is an accident for the company, not just in the down time getting the poor soul to the hospital and then finding a replacement while the person is out of commission. It goes much further than that! It is called 'Workman's Compensation' (at least in Canada, in other countries it may be called something different but it is an insurance all employers have to buy into, it is compulsory!). The premiums for this insurance are based on the type of business you have, if there are lots of accidents and it is dangerous, then the premiums are very high, and every accident that takes place in your company, yes, you guessed it, they go UP! Not just for that one employee who had the accident but for each of the employees within the whole company! So you are looking at a lot of dollars! And what makes the heart beat in an oil company? MONEY—Dollars! It breaks their hearts to have to cough up all those dollars! Too many accidents could almost put the oil company into cardiac arrest!

Scrutinize your business, take an eagle's view and search for where an accident could happen. Be Proactive and fix it! This is good management! I want **YOU** to be the Best Manager, taking your business to the top of your niche! How proud I am you have come this far, I know you have the tenacity to go the distance and make a difference in the world! The world needs more people like **YOU**!

9

WOW! YOU ARE GENERATING OIL! YOU CAN'T STOP THE FLOW!

Once you hit Oil it starts to Gush (Excitement)

The excitement on a drilling site when they know the well is just about to blow is incredible! The fellows at the rig phone all the other guys they have been working with, because everyone on site at the time the well blows gets a bonus! When the oil starts to gush out the top of that oil derrick, there is nothing quite so beautifully black! It just keeps spouting out the top and it just keeps raining down on those below. Being completely soaked in that black gold feels GOOD! It has been a long time coming and now it is here!

In business it is very much the same, for the exception of getting dirty black and a bit smelly. You work so very hard and then all of a sudden the lid comes off, you have done all the right things, sometimes you wonder if you are doing the right thing or if anyone will visit your site or buy your products or need your services. But about the time you are pondering this, the clogs in the big watch hit the right hour for the floodgates to open! It all has an order and a timeline. We may not know the exact timeline but if we get the order right, those floodgates will not be able to be closed. When the lid it taken off the pressure is such that you can't put it back on. But in reality, who would want to? Not me!

You know I talk about coaches a lot, which is because they are so very essential to whatever you are doing. They tell you what the next move might be, remember you are the one in control and it is your decision what that move will be, but a coach gives you options and helps guide to the right option. When you are coming close for the oil well of your business to blow, sit down and discuss what fame and fortune, can do and will do in your life. Talk about how you are going to manager this new life style. Make sure you go through every area of your life. Knowledge (and For-Knowledge is even better!) will be your saving grace, as you will know what to expect.

There are so many people who have won a lottery and within a short time end up worse off than before they won all that money! I know it is hard to understand, but it is true. These people have not had honest people to guide through all those pitfalls (that is even if they even thought of having someone help!) This is one big reason to start out in business with a GOOD coach, someone you can trust implicitly! Because when you hit that vein of oil or gold (or special product or your special service that everyone wants!) everyone will want to be your best friend and everyone will want you to invest in their schemes. This is where so many people come unstuck. 'No' has not been a word in their vocabulary, they feel mean if they do not help of give when someone asks. So often these people are conmen and they know all the right words to tickle your ears, to make things sound so right and compel you to hand over your money for their Ponzi scheme. I think I have said enough about this now, you have caught the drift and you are aware you have the right to say 'NO'. Because I give the authority to do so!

Red Adair—We Need YOU!

Excitement can turn into terror if the well cannot be tapped! Years ago there was a man who was a miracle worker when it came to difficult situations in the oil industry, his name—Red Adair! He was fearless in the face of trouble; his specialty was tapping off wells and fighting oil and gas well fires. I recall as a young person, there was a well that blew in the Algeria, they called it the Devil's Cigarette Lighter and it had been on fire for six months, finally after trying everything they knew to put out fires and failing, they called in Red Adair to finish the job! This was where Red's reputation began in earnest, he was the Hero of the oil and gas industry, his name was on everyone's lips and was a house hold name. From that point on he was heralded as 'THE OIL WELL FIREFIGHTER'.

While living in Britain, his name loomed to the forefront of every media. An Oil Rig in the North Sea was destroyed by an explosion in 1988; he and his Crew were the first firefighters on board. A few years later he and his men put out all the fires in Kuwait that the Iraqi military had started during Desert Storm. Now this man was a Texan. Everything in Texas is big, but Red Adair can only be majestically monstrous! He was Texas royalty!

In business, you need the tenacity and the fearlessness that Red Adair exuded. If you become the ingenious, skillful expert in your field as Red was in his, you will be sought after from those around the world. The work does not have to be dangerous like fighting raging fires, as not many are up to that kind of work. But what you need to be is someone who shines in what you do. If this is the case, there will come a day where someone will spout off praises of you and you will go 'viral'! Be the Best you can be, and all things will be added unto you!

All Bolted Down

After the oil well blows, the fire (if there is one) has been put out, things go back to normal. Everything has been bolted down and secured, it has been quite a roller coaster ride, almost every emotion has been experienced, excitement, joy, panic, fear, terror and finally relief.

Business will give you all those emotions in one way or another. Excitement and joy overcomes you when you first start with your new idea. The feeling of panic, wondering if you can get it all put together.

Then fear of not getting things going in time before the money runs out. Finally relief, when things start to return to normal. By this time you have hired those you need to help you accomplish the day to day tasks of the business, your heart beats a bit slower and you can breathe easier. Learning is an experience not to be missed, and experience is learning that gives you Character. Don't leave home without Character! The more Character you have the more you will be noticed, the more you are noticed, the greater you and your business become!

Welcome to your Place in the World! We all have been waiting for YOU!

Flowing through the Pipes

When the oil starts to flow through the pipeline, the money starts to roll in! For an oil company it has taken a lot of time and money to get them to this point. Once the oil flows it is worth it all as the oil just keeps coming out of the well. When you drive past an oil field you see many 'Donkeys' pumping the oil up from the wells, they just keep nodding their heads and with each nod, the cash register goes 'cha-ching'! The hard dirty work has been finished, and this donkey lazily goes about his business making the oil company very wealthy!

When your business starts to settle into a comfortable position, where you have people buying your products or services, and word of mouth has started to grow your client base to something just beyond your imagination, your cash register too will be singing that sweet little song!

Once it starts—it's almost impossible to Stop!

Once the ball start rolling, once the oil starts flowing, it is very difficult to stop. When people like what you have to offer, they will want more of everything you have then they will tell their friends and family about you. It doubles, then quadruples and then it just explodes. There is no way to stop this flow, if you continue to provide quality. This is a very lovely place to be. It has taken a lot of hard grueling work from you but it is now paying off, you deserve it all! Well Done My Friend! Tell me about your success. I would in turn love to interview you on 2O Radio let and my listeners enjoy hearing what good things can be done with a bit of fortitude and a lot of gumption!

Email me at Cheryl@2O-Radio.com

10

CLEANING UP THE SITE—GIVING BACK!

After Things have Settled Down

After the big rush of the gusher, and all the time lead-
ing up to it, life was pretty busy and exciting, but once
the well has been capped off and a pump has been
placed on it, things settle down, the site starts to look
more orderly, the company takes the time to disman-
tle the rig carefully and transport it to the next drilling
site and it starts over in a new place. The old site becomes like a brood mare, which once was a racehorse,
who now has been put out to pasture, no longer needing the speed, hard work and training, but allowing
her to live gently on the land producing great profits
through her offspring. The old well site now produces
great profits through that wonderful black gold it just
naturally keeps pumping up.

When your business gets to this point, you can take a
breather, it is time to relax and enjoy the profits of your
hard work. You do have to keep an eye on your numbers,

so you know where the company is at and fly over to get the eagle's view making sure everything is in order, but you have set it all in motion and it is not going to stop!

Starting to Restore and Reclaim
Where you have been!

Oil companies have departments for the soul purpose of restoration and reclamation. When the derrick and site office and other paraphernalia used to drill the well have been removed to the new site, restoration begins on the old site. They try to put the land back to as close to how it was before they arrived. I know the companies that have drilled on our land have worked hard to make sure that every little detail is looked after. They have planted grass seed, and found that there was no rain that year so it started to grow but shriveled and died, the next year they came back and re-seeded making sure the grass came back. They bend over backwards to make the landowners happy, and they do not stop until they are.

A lesson for a business owner, bend over backwards to make your clients happy. It costs seven times more to acquire a new customer than it does to keep an old one. Give them special little gifts, the cost is not a factor in this case, it can be as small as a phone call from you personally or from one of your staff. A man I know who has a number of huge businesses, you would know the names of the businesses if I told you, personally phones 4 to 5 clients a day, just to say hello and ask how their day is going. The phone calls are not more than 5 minutes, but in doing this he has re-established the relationship with that person. He has restored good will to all his businesses! Think of a few little things that can make a huge impact on your clients and in turn on your company!

Time to make a Difference—Where

When an oil company finishes the drilling activity at the site, it is time to make a difference to the community it has been working in. I am not sure who decides what the company is going to do, but someone has looked at the needs of the community and they fund a project for that community. It is called giving back or paying it forward. Everyone benefits. Sometimes it might be equipment for a youth group other times if there are more than one well in the community, it might be a recreation center or a skating arena.

When you have benefited through your business, be grateful for all you have been able to achieve and give back to those who have been part of your success. Don't stop there, give to those who are in great need, a charity who works in overseas countries where there is no way, the people can make a living for any number of reasons, famine, drought, pestilents, wars and terrorism. I'm sure there are many more reasons. But for whatever reason some one is hungry or needs medical care and we can give it for a few dollars, is that not worth every cent, to know some child goes to bed with a full tummy, or someone has their eye sight restored. Just a thought, that I leave with you.

At the Site

Oil companies often leave behind jobs for the local people. This injects money back into the community.

This makes them heroes! Possibly the pay is less than having to keep one of their staff manning that position, with housing and whatever other benefit are required to keep them in a remote area (not in a city!) But people in the community are only too thankful for the opportunity of the work, which most likely pays more than the businesses in that community.

The oil company will train the person for the job either onsite or will pay for them to go get the training where it is offered. Oil companies are very fair and good employers.

A thought for you, think of things that you do not have time for or just don't enjoy doing. There are people in your neighborhood that would love the work, they are capable and for some reason they do not a job. What about someone to do your gardening, (in my area) snow shoveling, someone to do your grocery shopping, someone to clean your windows? The list of things is endless. Remember, it is time to take a bit more time for yourself and you cannot do everything, as much as you think you can! Start to enjoy the new life you are creating!

With the People and Wildlife (And it was Good!)

Oil companies try to restore all they have taken from the land. They are ever mindful of the wildlife and the habitat that it lives in. They try to make a difference in the lives of the people where they have been drilling, by paying them rent for the well sites and offering them paid positions. They give to the community, not only money for projects but will volunteer their time to make sure the project is a success.

Giving back is good business. Sharing a little of what we have with those who have nothing, is just plain good!

I hope to meet you one day, so you can tell me all that you have been able to accomplish and a few stories of how you have been able to change someone's life.

It has been my pleasure to spend this time with you. Thank you!

I look forward to one day to sitting down and enjoy a cup of tea with you. Let's make it some 'Texas Tea'

Go to www.Extra-OrdinaryConnections.com to find real people that excel in their professions and in this case look under 'Marketing'.

A Coach is waiting for you, and you can find him or her at www.Extra-OrdinaryConnections.com look under 'Coaches'.

Email me at cheryl@cherylbutterworth.com